Ten
for /

ex libris

Candlestick Press

Published by:
Candlestick Press,
Diversity House, 72 Nottingham Road, Arnold, Nottingham UK NG5 6LF
www.candlestickpress.co.uk

Design and typesetting by Craig Twigg

Printed by Ratcliff & Roper Print Group, Nottinghamshire, UK

Selection © Di Slaney and Katharine Towers

Introduction © Katharine Towers

Cover illustration © Alexandra Buckle, 2020
www.alexandrabuckle.co.uk

Candlestick Press monogram © Barbara Shaw, 2008

© Candlestick Press, 2020

ISBN 978 1 907598 98 2

Acknowledgements

The poems in this pamphlet are reprinted from the following books, all by
permission of the publishers listed unless stated otherwise. Every effort has
been made to trace the copyright holders of the poems published in this book.
The editors and publisher apologise if any material has been included without
permission or without the appropriate acknowledgement, and would be glad to be
told of anyone who has not been consulted.

Thanks are due to all the copyright holders cited below for their kind permission:

Maggie Dietz, *That Kind of Happy* (University of Chicago Press, 2016)
cleared through the Copyright Clearance Center. Ted Kooser, *Weather Central*
(University of Pittsburgh Press, 1994) © 1994, reprinted with permissions of
University of Pittsburgh Press. Jane Hirshfield, *After* (Bloodaxe Books, 2006;
HarperCollins, 2006) www.bloodaxebooks.com. Freya Manfred, *My Only
Home* (Red Dragonfly, 2015) used with kind permission of the author. Vinode B
Ramgopal, poem first published in this anthology. RS Thomas, poem taken from
A Book of Nature Poems, ed. William Cole (Viking Press, 1969) by permission of
Bloodaxe Books on behalf of the Estate of RS Thomas.

All permissions cleared courtesy of Swift Permissions
swiftpermissions@gmail.com

Where poets are no longer living, their dates are given.

Introduction

Autumn must be one of poetry's favourite seasons. This mini anthology seeks to capture the subtle and sometimes melancholy music of a time when the year seems to gather its thoughts and offers up its work.

Of course, there is "mellow fruitfulness" – not only in Keats' canonical poem (one that we absolutely couldn't do without!) but also in the form of Freya Manfred's old man enjoying a juicy pear picked from the tree he planted years ago. We find falling leaves in Emily Brontë's exquisite short lyric, and farmers ploughing fields and fixing their boundary walls in Vinode B Ramgopal's paean to the season he describes as "a treasury / of breakage and release".

But it's certainly not all golden trees and shining berries; autumn also has a raw edge. In Jane Hirshfield's tender and moving poem about endings, the river is "each day a full measure colder". For Maggie Dietz, the arrival of November brings a sky "like hardened plaster" although her poem strikes a note of feisty defiance.

The Lebanese-American poet Kahlil Gibran is whimsically mystical in his prose poem 'Said a Blade of Grass.' An imagined conversation between a blade of grass and a falling leaf becomes a sly meditation on nature's endless cycle of renewal; without autumn there can be no spring.

Amy Lowell's 'September, 1918' encapsulates a bitter-sweet moment in time in its eighteen lines. The beauty of autumn will only be fully savoured when the war is over; for now its glories must be kept safe in a poem.

This is perhaps the quiet message of our selection: look hard and try to memorise the beauty you see because winter will be long and – as RS Thomas observes – the mind will need this photograph.

Katharine Towers

The Heat of Autumn

The heat of autumn
is different from the heat of summer.
One ripens apples, the other turns them to cider.
One is a dock you walk out on,
the other the spine of a thin swimming horse
and the river each day a full measure colder.
A man with cancer leaves his wife for his lover.
Before he goes she straightens his belts in the closet,
rearranges the socks and sweaters inside the dresser
by color. That's autumn heat:
her hand placing silver buckles with silver,
gold buckles with gold, setting each
on the hook it belongs on in a closet soon to be empty,
and calling it pleasure.

Jane Hirshfield

Said a Blade of Grass

Said a blade of grass to an autumn leaf, "You make such a noise falling! You scatter all my winter dreams."

Said the leaf indignant, "Low-born and low-dwelling! Songless, peevish thing! You live not in the upper air and you cannot tell the sound of singing."

Then the autumn leaf lay down upon the earth and slept. And when spring came she waked again – and she was a blade of grass.

And when it was autumn and her winter sleep was upon her, and above her through all the air the leaves were falling, she muttered to herself, "O these autumn leaves! They make such noise! They scatter all my winter dreams."

Kahlil Gibran (1883 – 1931)

Fall Leaves Fall

Fall leaves fall die flowers away
Lengthen night and shorten day
Every leaf speaks bliss to me
Fluttering from the autumn tree
I shall smile when wreaths of snow
Blossom where the rose should grow
I shall sing when night's decay
Ushers in a drearier day

Emily Brontë (1818 – 1848)

The Invitation of Autumn

We come to autumn
On thrones of sealed air
Wanderers at windows,
Gazing on country roads
As they bend over hills

And passing tractors resting
In fields of turned clay
As birds call out south
On fingers of marmalade,
We watch winter
Steal November
And summer reach up
To festivals of fall.

Sometimes we stop to study
Husbandry outdoors,
Tidying boundaries,
Raising fallen stones,
In places where time
Is tethered to a sturdy pole.

And sometimes smiling
At naïve flowers
Blossoming in soughs
Of renegade air
We lower windows
To let in the chemist.

But so few of us
Will open the door
And step off the throne
Accepting this invitation
To scatter the senses
See the wind inhale,
Touch the geese calls
Taste the yielding paths
Down to the fields
In this treasury
Of breakage and release.

Vinode B Ramgopal

Green Pear Tree in September

On a hill overlooking the Rock River
my father's pear tree shimmers,
in perfect peace,
covered with hundreds of ripe pears
with pert tops, plump bottoms,
and long curved leaves.
Until the green-haloed tree
rose up and sang hello,
I had forgotten...
He planted it twelve years ago,
when he was seventy-three,
so that in September
he could stroll down
with the sound of the crickets
rising and falling around him,
and stand, naked to the waist,
slightly bent, sucking juice
from a ripe pear.

Freya Manfred

To Autumn

Season of mists and mellow fruitfulness,
  Close bosom-friend of the maturing sun;
Conspiring with him how to load and bless
  With fruit the vines that round the thatch-eves run;
To bend with apples the moss'd cottage-trees,
  And fill all fruit with ripeness to the core;
    To swell the gourd, and plump the hazel shells
  With a sweet kernel; to set budding more,
And still more, later flowers for the bees,
Until they think warm days will never cease,
    For Summer has o'er-brimm'd their clammy cells.

Who hath not seen thee oft amid thy store?
  Sometimes whoever seeks abroad may find
Thee sitting careless on a granary floor,
  Thy hair soft-lifted by the winnowing wind;
Or on a half-reap'd furrow sound asleep,
  Drows'd with the fume of poppies, while thy hook
    Spares the next swath and all its twined flowers:
And sometimes like a gleaner thou dost keep
  Steady thy laden head across a brook;
  Or by a cyder-press, with patient look,
    Thou watchest the last oozings hours by hours.

Where are the songs of Spring? Ay, where are they?
  Think not of them, thou hast thy music too,–
While barred clouds bloom the soft-dying day,
  And touch the stubble-plains with rosy hue;
Then in a wailful choir the small gnats mourn
  Among the river sallows, borne aloft
    Or sinking as the light wind lives or dies;
And full-grown lambs loud bleat from hilly bourn;
  Hedge-crickets sing; and now with treble soft
  The red-breast whistles from a garden-croft;
    And gathering swallows twitter in the skies.

John Keats (1795 – 1821)

September, 1918

This afternoon was the colour of water falling through sunlight;
The trees glittered with the tumbling of leaves;
The sidewalks shone like alleys of dropped maple leaves,
And the houses ran along them laughing out of square, open windows.
Under a tree in the park,
Two little boys, lying flat on their faces,
Were carefully gathering red berries
To put in a pasteboard box.
Some day there will be no war,
Then I shall take out this afternoon
And turn it in my fingers,
And remark the sweet taste of it upon my palate,
And note the crisp variety of its flights of leaves.
To-day I can only gather it
And put it into my lunch-box,
For I have time for nothing
But the endeavour to balance myself
Upon a broken world.

Amy Lowell (1874 – 1925)

A Letter in October

Dawn comes later and later now,
and I, who only a month ago
could sit with coffee every morning
watching the light walk down the hill
to the edge of the pond and place
a doe there, shyly drinking,

then see the light step out upon
the water, sowing reflections
to either side – a garden
of trees that grew as if by magic –
now see no more than my face,
mirrored by darkness, pale and odd,

startled by time. While I slept,
night in its thick winter jacket
bridled the doe with a twist
of wet leaves and led her away,
then brought its black horse with harness
that creaked like a cricket, and turned

the water garden under. I woke,
and at the waiting window found
the curtains open to my open face;
beyond me, darkness. And I,
who only wished to keep looking out,
must now keep looking in.

Ted Kooser

November

Show's over, folks. And didn't October do
A bang-up job? Crisp breezes, full-throated cries
Of migrating geese, low-floating coral moon.

Nothing left but fool's gold in the trees.
Did I love it enough, the full-throttle foliage,
While it lasted? Was I dazzled? The bees

Have up and quit their last-ditch flights of forage
And gone to shiver in their winter clusters.
Field mice hit the barns, big squirrels gorge

On busted chestnuts. A sky like hardened plaster
Hovers. The pasty river, its next of kin,
Coughs up reed grass fat as feather dusters.

Even the swarms of kids have given in
To winter's big excuse, boxed-in allure:
TVs ricochet light behind pulled curtains.

The days throw up a closed sign around four.
The hapless customer who'd wanted something
Arrives to find lights out, a bolted door.

Maggie Dietz

A Day in Autumn

It will not always be like this,
The air windless, a few last
Leaves adding their decoration
To the trees' shoulders, braiding the cuffs
Of the boughs with gold; a bird preening

In the lawn's mirror. Having looked up
From the day's chores, pause a minute,
Let the mind take its photograph
Of the bright scene, something to wear
Against the heart in the long cold.

RS Thomas (1913 – 2000)